W9-ATF-070

DATE			
		2/1	

THE STORY OF CLOCKS AND CALENDARS:
MARKING A MILLENNIUM

BY **BETSY MAESTRO**
ILLUSTRATED BY **GIULIO MAESTRO**

LOTHROP, LEE & SHEPARD BOOKS
New York

"So what is time? If no one asks me, I know; if they ask and I try to explain, I do not know."
—St. Augustine

Note: Throughout this book the indications BC (Before Christ) and AD (*Anno Domini*, in the Year of Our Lord) are used to clarify dates because they are the most commonly known and widely used terms. They are, however, religious terms used only in conjunction with the Gregorian calendar. The terms BCE (Before the Common Era) and CE (Common Era) are becoming more widespread, as they convey a more multicultural approach to calendars and historic dating.

Pencil, colored pencils, ink, and watercolors were used for the full-color illustrations. The text type is 13-point Lucida Sans.

Text copyright © 1999 by Betsy Maestro   Illustrations copyright © 1999 by Giulio Maestro

Published by Lothrop, Lee & Shepard Books, an imprint of Morrow Junior Books, a division of William Morrow and Company, Inc., 1350 Avenue of the Americas, New York, NY 10019   www.williammorrow.com

Printed in Singapore at Tien Wah Press.

10 9 8 7 6 5 4

Library of Congress Cataloging-in-Publication Data
Maestro, Betsy.
The story of clocks and calendars: marking a millennium / Betsy Maestro; illustrated by Giulio Maestro.
p. cm.
Includes index.
Summary: Discusses the year 2000 as a milestone marking two thousand years
of human achievement, as a threshold leading into a new millennium, and
as an important anniversary of the birth of Jesus Christ.
ISBN 0-688-14548-5 (trade)—ISBN 0-688-14549-3 (library)
1. Two thousand, AD—Juvenile literature.   2. Millennium—Juvenile literature.
3. Calendar—History—Juvenile literature.   [1. Two thousand, AD.   2. Millennium.
3. Calendar.]   I. Maestro, Giulio, ill.   II. Title.   CB161.M333   1999   909.83—dc21
98-21305   CIP AC

FOR AS LONG AS ANYONE CAN REMEMBER, people have thought of the year 2000 as "the future"—a time way ahead of us, when somehow things would be different and new. Stories set in the year 2000 and beyond have always been part of science fiction—something from the imagination. Now that future is a reality.

Although January 1, 2001, officially begins the new millennium, the festivities started a year before that date, when New Year's Eve was celebrated, December 31, 1999. People all over the world looked forward to this rare event with great excitement. But what makes this date and time so special? What is all the fuss about?

The year 2000 is both a great milestone, a time to mark two thousand years of human achievement, and a historic beginning, the entry into a new thousand-year period—a new millennium. It is also an important time for people of the Christian religion, who are celebrating the two-thousand-year anniversary of the birth of Jesus Christ.

3

People mark the passing of time by counting the years. Each year we celebrate birthdays and anniversaries, counting the years since the people we know were born or married. Even one year can seem like a very long time, so the passing of one hundred years—a century—has always been given special notice. A thousand years is ten times as long as a century, so a new millennium is a truly awesome event.

But even though the year 2000 seems very important to us, it is really only a tiny part of the long story of time, where a year is shorter than the blink of an eye. A millennium is a very long time in human history but only a short time in the history of our planet and universe.

The young earth and moon, hundreds of millions of years ago

Our universe is probably at least twelve billion years old, and our earth is about four and a half billion years old. It is difficult for us to imagine such long periods of time. A billion is a really large number—more than a hundred, more than a thousand, more than a million. A billion years is made up of one million millennia.

So our earth has lived through millions of millennia, and scientists now think that *Homo sapiens*—humans like us—could possibly have lived on earth for as many as two hundred millennia. Why, then, is everyone making such a fuss about the year 2000? And how can this be only the year 2000 when our earth is so much older and people have been around for such a long time?

Early cave dwellers more than a hundred thousand years ago

The answer is that it is only the year 2000 on the Gregorian calendar—the calendar most people use. There are many other calendars. The year 2000 began in the year 5760 on the Hebrew calendar and in 1420 on the Muslim calendar. It is 4698 on the Chinese calendar. So what year is it really? There is no one answer. It depends on what calendar you use and how long ago your calendar began counting the years. But the Gregorian calendar is the standard calendar used around the world, and for everyone who uses that calendar, it is the year 2000.

A calendar is one way to keep track of time. We look at it every day to see what day, month, or year it is. A clock also helps us to measure time. We look at it to see if it's time for school or soccer practice or bed. Everyone needs to know what time it is, so clocks and calendars are important in our lives.

But time means different things to different people. For little children a year may seem endless when they're waiting for their next birthday. Busy adults sometimes feel that time is going too fast; they never have enough time to get everything done. Time always seems to hurry by when you are having fun, and slow down when you are bored or unhappy. An athlete can win or lose by a hundredth of a second, while most of us don't have to worry about seconds at all.

Often we think of time as a group of minutes, hours, days, months, or years. A period of time might be "the first race," "the last inning," or "summer vacation." Sometimes we think of time as many connected happenings, like "colonial times" or "school days." Some periods of time—"since the beginning of the earth" or "during the Ice Age"—may be longer than what we can even imagine.

For scientists time is a dimension like length and mass—something that can be measured but doesn't always remain the same. Astronomers may measure time by astronomical events such as a solar eclipse. The period of rule by a great king may be a unit of time for an historian.

Time is something of a riddle or mystery. It seems easy to understand when we think of clocks and calendars. But when we try to explain exactly what time is, we can't really say.

Although humans a lot like us may have lived on earth for two hundred thousand years, it is hard to learn about the lives of the earliest people. Historic time—the period that we know a lot about—began only about four to five thousand years ago, when people learned to write and record events. Archaeologists have helped us learn about prehistory by digging up and studying the remains of ancient people and their belongings.

An archaeologist uncovers fragments of ancient pottery.

Left page: A solar eclipse, as seen at the site of the McMath solar telescope in Arizona

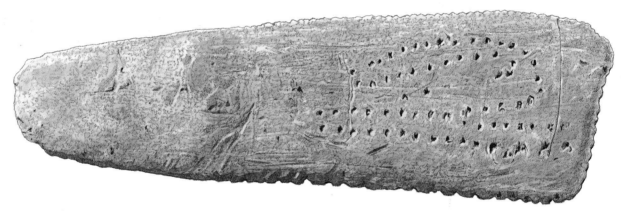

The first humans were hunters and gatherers. They got their food by killing animals and gathering edible greens and fruits. Over time people noticed that many natural events, like the rising and setting of the sun and the changing of the seasons, occurred over and over again. They began to expect these same events to happen once more. This ability made it possible for people to plan their activities according to nature's changes. They learned to collect and store berries and nuts before the winter came, and to follow animals as they migrated with the seasons.

These early humans had little use for very small units of time like minutes and seconds. They watched the sun and moon to tell the time of day or night. The changing seasons told them what time of year it was. Sometimes they kept track of the passing months and years by carving scratches on sticks, stones, or pieces of bone. These first calendars were very crude and simple. Archaeologists have found "calendar sticks" that may be more than thirty thousand years old.

Left: An ancient African calendar stick made of bone

Above: These marks carved into bone seem to be a record of the phases of the moon, as seen over several months.

Carved about 10,000 BC, this bone may
be the world's oldest solar calendar.

Over many thousands of years people began to change the way they
lived. They learned to grow their own food by planting seeds and harvesting
the plants that grew. As they became better farmers, they began to settle
down in one place. They relied less on hunting as they started to raise animals
for food themselves.

These early farmers depended on and often worshiped the sun, which
they saw as the source of all life. They began to notice that as the seasons
changed, so did the location of the sun in the sky. They may have calculated
the length of a year by watching and recording the sun's positions.

Farming began thousands of years
ago in the Middle East.

People were equally fascinated by the moon. Over a period of many days, the moon changed its shape a little each night, until it looked the way it had when the cycle began. Then the whole process would happen all over again. Ancient astronomers—those who studied the skies—knew ahead of time when there would be a full moon.

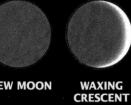

| NEW MOON | WAXING CRESCENT | FIRST QUARTER | WAXING GIBBOUS | FULL MOON | WANING GIBBOUS | LAST QUARTER | WANING CRESCENT | NEW MOON |

Hundreds of standing stones, erected with great precision between 6000 and 1500 BC, have been found in many places around the world, particularly in northern Europe. The stones sometimes stand alone and are sometimes set in great circles. They were often placed so that they would mark the points of sunrise or sunset on the horizon at different times of the year. The chosen days were usually the summer and winter solstices, which are the longest and shortest days of the year, and the equinoxes at the beginning of spring and fall, when day and night are of equal length. Many ancient festivals and rituals were planned around these special days, which marked the beginnings of the four seasons.

The summer solstice sunrise at Stonehenge, England

Decorative panels in the Sumerian style show scenes of agriculture.

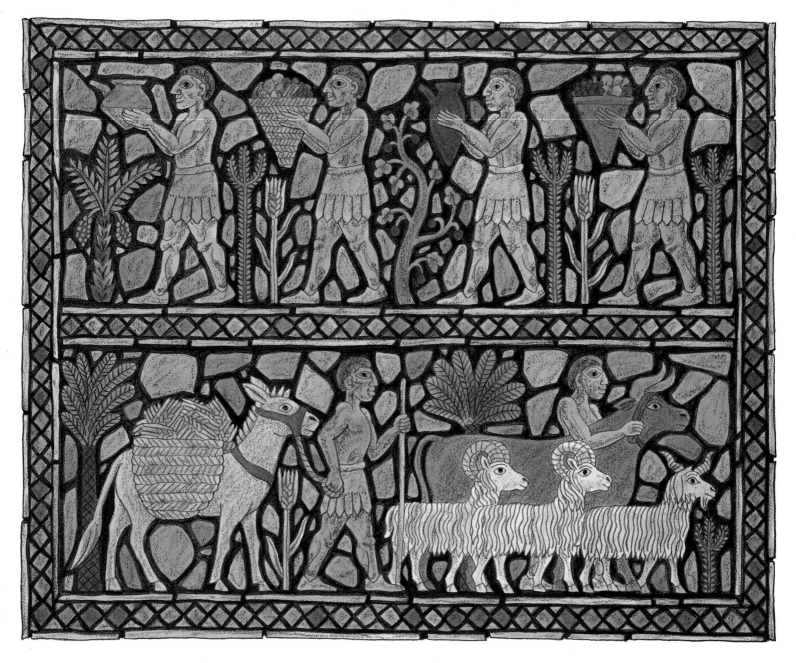

The earliest written calendars were lunar—based on the cycles of the moon. The Sumerians, who lived in the ancient Near East in a place called Mesopotamia, were probably the first to devise such a calendar, about five thousand years ago. They used their calendar to plan the planting and harvesting of crops. The calendar had two seasons—summer and winter— and was divided into twelve months for the twelve lunar cycles in the year. Each lunar month had twenty-nine or thirty days, based on their observations of the moon. Sumerian astronomers were the first to keep written records of what they learned about the heavens.

Flood Time

The three seasons of the Egyptian year

Planting Time

Harvest Time

The ancient Egyptians also used a lunar calendar to help plan their farming year. The flooding of the Nile River each year was a very important event for the Egyptians. The floods brought rich new soil down from the highlands, changing desert into farmland. So the Egyptian new year started at the time of the first new moon after the spring floods.

The Egyptian calendar had only 360 days. But since this didn't exactly match the seasonal year, the Egyptians eventually realized that their lunar year was too short. They had to keep adding extra days to keep pace with the seasons.

Flood time along the Nile River

So around 2772 BC, the Egyptians replaced their lunar calendar with the world's first solar calendar, which was more accurate. The solar year is based on the time it takes for the earth to make one complete trip around the sun—almost exactly 365 days—though ancient people thought it was the sun moving around the earth. The days of all the moon's cycles in a year don't add up to 365, but rather to 354, eleven days shorter than the solar year. So calendars based on the moon don't keep time with the seasons. In their new calendar, the Egyptians started each new year with the rising of the star Sirius, which occurs at the same time every year, just before the spring floods.

Planting Time

Harvest Time

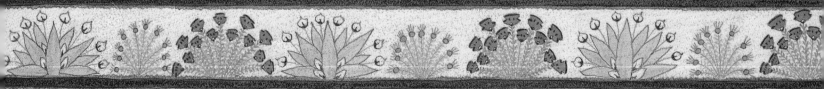

About 1750 BC, the Babylonians, another ancient people in the Near East, made some changes to the calendar they inherited from the Sumerians. The Babylonians made this lunar calendar work by adding an extra month every few years. They also made some changes that we still use today. Using a very advanced number system based on sixty, they divided the day into twenty-four hours, the hour into sixty minutes, and the minute into sixty seconds.

The Babylonians recorded astronomical observations on clay tablets.

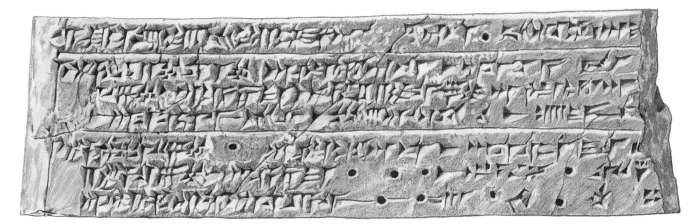

BABYLONIAN ASTRONOMICAL SYMBOLS

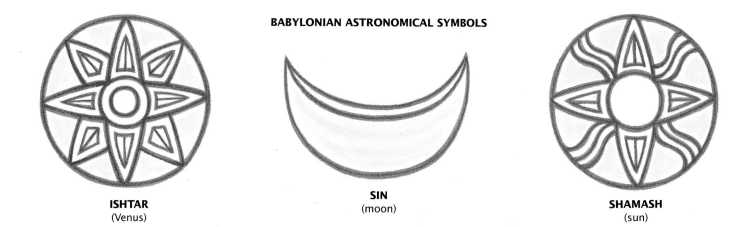

ISHTAR
(Venus)

SIN
(moon)

SHAMASH
(sun)

The Babylonians gave the week seven days, which they named after the sun (Shamash), the moon (Sin), and five bright "stars," which were really planets (Nergal, Nabu, Marduk, Ishtar, and Ninurta). Later the Romans renamed the days after Roman gods: Sol, Luna, Mars, Mercury, Jupiter, Venus, and Saturn. Our day names are from the Anglo-Saxon words for the same gods: Sun (Sunday), Moon (Monday), Tiw (Tuesday), Woden (Wednesday), Thor (Thursday), Frigg (Friday), and Saturn (Saturday).

The ancient Chinese also used a lunar calendar, probably beginning in 1953 BC. In that year a rare celestial event occurred. The sun, the moon, and the five planets that look like bright stars all lined up in the eastern sky at dawn. Many scholars now believe that this year became the basis for the Chinese calendar.

The Chinese divided the twelve lunar months into twenty-four periods related to their farming year. The name of each division described something that happened at that time of year. Spring included Rain Water, Excited Insects, and Great Rains. In summer there were Grain Fills, Slight Heat, and Great Heat. Fall included White Dew and Descent of Frost, and winter had Great Snow and Severe Cold.

18

But all lunar calendars still had the same problem that the Egyptians and others had long struggled with—the shorter lunar year caused the calendar eventually to get out of step with the seasons. In the fifth century BC, a Greek astronomer named Meton came up with a solution. The Metonic Cycle brought lunar and solar calendars in step by adding seven months during each nineteen-year period.

The Greeks made contributions to astronomy as well as to calendars. Although like most ancient peoples they believed that all celestial bodies traveled around the earth, they were the first to proclaim that the earth was round, and that it was not standing still but spinning around. They mapped the positions of a thousand stars and invented ways of measuring their brightness and distance from the earth.

An Arab astrolabe from the eleventh century AD

Early Greek astronomers used astrolabes to map the positions of the stars.

19

Across the ocean in the Americas, Maya astronomers began to watch the heavens too. Later they built observatories and mapped the movements of the sun, moon, planets, and stars with remarkable accuracy. They calculated the length of the solar year to be 365.2420 days. Using modern technology, scientists today have determined the exact length of a solar year to be 365.2422 days—a difference of only seconds from the Maya number figured so long ago.

The Maya developed an advanced number system—one of the first to include a symbol for the concept of zero. They could work with very large numbers quickly and easily, an ability they needed for their extremely complex calendar calculations. Their calendar consisted of two separate cycles—a 260-day sacred cycle used for religious purposes, and a 365-day solar cycle. Every fifty-two years exactly, the two cycles came together and began again at the same moment. The Maya also kept a "Long Count" that indicated the number of days they believed had passed since the creation of the world. On the Gregorian calendar, Maya creation would have occurred on August 13, 3114 BC.

The Maya also practiced astrology, believing that the position of celestial bodies influenced their daily lives. They used these observations along with their calendar to predict the future as well as to determine the best times for all actions in their daily lives.

MONTH NAMES AND NUMBERS

1. POP 2. UO 3. ZIP 4. ZOTZ 5. TZEC 6. XUL 7. YAXKIN

8. MOL 9. CHEN 10. YAX 11. ZAC 12. CEH 13. MAC 14. KANKIN

15. MUAN 16. PAX 17. KAYAB 18. CUMKU 19. UAYEB

THE MONTHS

The 365-day cycle had eighteen months of twenty days each, with an extra five-day period called Uayeb at the end. The Maya knew that this "Vague Year" did not exactly equal a solar year.

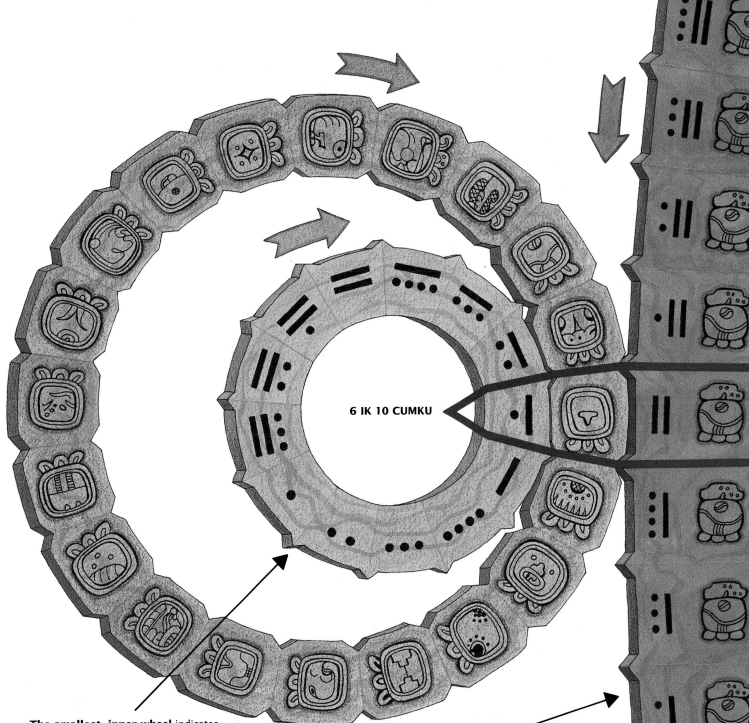

6 IK 10 CUMKU

The smallest, inner wheel indicates day numbers from one to thirteen.

These two wheels together represent the 260-day sacred cycle of twenty months of thirteen days.

The outer, middle-sized wheel shows the glyphs, or symbols, for the twenty day names.

Part of **the largest wheel** is displayed on the right. This wheel represents the 365-day solar cycle—eighteen months of twenty days each plus the five days of Uayeb.

As these wheels turn and mesh, the two calendars combine. Each particular combination of the four elements—sacred day name, number, solar month, and solar day—occurs only once every fifty-two years. The day shown here is **6 IK 10 CUMKU.**

LIBRA

VIRGO

SCORPIUS

The Maya were not the first people to practice astrology. In India, astrology may have been practiced as early as 6500 BC. The ancient Chinese, Egyptians, and Babylonians also watched the heavens for signs that would guide them in making important decisions. The Babylonians mapped the night sky and divided it into twelve equal sections with a group of stars called a constellation in each. They created the diagram that we know today as the zodiac, and used it to predict the future.

ARIES

PISCES

TAURUS

GEMINI

LEO

CANCER

The ancient Romans adopted the zodiac and made it their own. Priest-astronomers also watched the heavens for the first sign of the new moon in order to declare the beginning of each new month of the Roman calendar year. The first days of the months came to be called Kalends, or Calends, after the Latin word *calare,* which means "to announce or call out." This is how we got our word *calendar.*

THE ROMAN ZODIAC

AQUARIUS

SAGITTARIUS

CAPRICORNUS

The first Roman calendars were borrowed from the Greek lunar calendar. The year had only ten months, beginning with the spring month of Marius (our March). It was followed by Aprilis (April), Maius (May), Junius (June), Quintilis (meaning fifth), Sextilis (sixth), September (seventh), October (eighth), November (ninth), and December (tenth). All this made perfect sense until sometime at the end of the seventh century BC, when the Roman emperor Numa Pompilius added two extra months to bring the lunar calendar back in step with the solar seasons. The new months—Januarius (January) and Februarius (February)—later became the first and second months, making the names Quintilis through December seem foolish. Later on, two other Roman emperors, Julius Caesar and Augustus Caesar, renamed Quintilis and Sextilis after themselves. The two months became Julius and Augustus—our July and August.

THE ROMAN FORUM
Many public buildings were located around a large plaza where Roman officials often gave speeches and discussed events and issues of the day.

A portrait of Julius Caesar
on a Roman coin

The addition of extra months did not fix the Roman calendar for long. Politics often got in the way of calendar progress. Roman senators sometimes voted to add extra months to the calendar in order to give themselves a longer term of office. The calendar year slowly lost pace with the seasons. Winter was coming when the calendar said it was fall. When it should have been summer, the calendar said spring.

By the time Julius Caesar came to power in 46 BC, the calendar needed major adjustment. After consulting a Greek astronomer named Sosigenes, Caesar ordered the following changes to the Roman calendar:

♦ The lunar calendar would be replaced with a solar one.
♦ The year would have 365¼ days instead of 365.
♦ The year would begin in January and have twelve months of fixed length.
♦ An extra day would be added every four years in the month of February.
♦ The months of January, March, May, July, September, and November would all have thirty-one days. All the other months would have thirty except February, which would have twenty-nine or thirty.

In addition, to restore the seasons to their proper places, Julius Caesar added eighty days to the current year. So the year 46 BC had 445 days. It became known as *Annus Confusionus*—the Year of Confusion!

Nineteen years later, in 27 BC, the emperor Augustus became ruler of Rome. After Julius Caesar's death, the extra day had been inserted incorrectly every three years instead of every four, so the calendar was in need of adjustment again. Augustus corrected for this mistake, then added some changes of his own. Since Julius had renamed a month after himself, Augustus did the same. But July (Julius's month) had thirty-one days while August (Augustus's month) had only thirty. So Augustus borrowed a day from February to add to his month, making February a twenty-eight-day month. Then he changed the number of days in September and November to thirty and gave October and December thirty-one.

JULIAN CALENDAR DURING THE REIGN OF AUGUSTUS (27 BC–AD 14)

C = Calends, 1st day; N = Nones, 5th or 7th day; I = Ides, 13th or 15th day;
* = 1 extra day every 4 years

JANUARIUS

I	II	III	IV	V	VI	VII
C	2	3	4	N	6	7
8	9	10	11	12	I	14
15	16	17	18	19	20	21
22	23	24	25	26	27	28
29	30	31				

FEBRUARIUS

I	II	III	IV	V	VI	VII
			C	2	3	4
N	6	7	8	9	10	11
12	I	14	15	16	17	18
19	20	21	22	23	24	25
26	27	28	*			

MARTIUS

I	II	III	IV	V	VI	VII
			C	2	3	4
5	6	N	8	9	10	11
12	13	14	I	16	17	18
19	20	21	22	23	24	25
26	27	28	29	30	31	

APRILIS

I	II	III	IV	V	VI	VII
						C
2	3	4	N	6	7	8
9	10	11	12	I	14	15
16	17	18	19	20	21	22
23	24	25	26	27	28	29
30						

MAIUS

I	II	III	IV	V	VI	VII
	C	2	3	4	5	6
N	8	9	10	11	12	13
14	I	16	17	18	19	20
21	22	23	24	25	26	27
28	29	30	31			

JUNIUS

I	II	III	IV	V	VI	VII
			C	2	3	
4	N	6	7	8	9	10
11	12	I	14	15	16	17
18	19	20	21	22	23	24
25	26	27	28	29	30	

JULIUS

I	II	III	IV	V	VI	VII
						C
2	3	4	5	6	N	8
9	10	11	12	13	14	I
16	17	18	19	20	21	22
23	24	25	26	27	28	29
30	31					

AUGUSTUS

I	II	III	IV	V	VI	VII
	C	2	3	4	N	
6	7	8	9	10	11	12
I	14	15	16	17	18	19
20	21	22	23	24	25	26
27	28	29	30	31		

SEPTEMBER

I	II	III	IV	V	VI	VII
					C	2
3	4	N	6	7	8	9
10	11	12	I	14	15	16
17	18	19	20	21	22	23
24	25	26	27	28	29	30

OCTOBER

I	II	III	IV	V	VI	VII
C	2	3	4	5	6	N
8	9	10	11	12	13	14
I	16	17	18	19	20	21
22	23	24	25	26	27	28
29	30	31				

NOVEMBER

I	II	III	IV	V	VI	VII
		C	2	3	4	
N	6	7	8	9	10	11
12	I	14	15	16	17	18
19	20	21	22	23	24	25
26	27	28	29	30		

DECEMBER

I	II	III	IV	V	VI	VII
					C	2
3	4	N	6	7	8	9
10	11	12	I	14	15	16
17	18	19	20	21	22	23
24	25	26	27	28	29	30
31						

More than five hundred years later, in AD 525, a Catholic monk named Dionysius Exiguus was asked to fix the calendar so that Christians all over the world would celebrate Easter on the same day. An astronomer and mathematician, Dionysius calculated what he thought to be the birth date of Jesus. He made this day the starting date for the Christian calendar. So the year 1 BC (Before Christ) was followed by the year AD 1 (*Anno Domini,* in the Year of Our Lord).

The calendar Dionysius worked on was the same one that Julius Caesar had fixed hundreds of years before. It is called the Julian calendar, and despite all the changing and confusion, it was easy to use and really quite accurate, losing only about one day every 128 years.

The Julian calendar was used in Europe for more than fifteen hundred years. However, over all those years, the one-day error grew to more than ten days. By the year 1582, the Catholic Church needed to act to end an embarrassing situation: Easter was being celebrated at the wrong time.

So Pope Gregory XIII, with the help of an astronomer-mathematician named Clavius, ordered some new changes. First, he eliminated ten days from that year's calendar: Thursday, October 4, 1582, was followed by Friday, October 15, 1582. Then, since the old Julian calendar was still not accurate enough, he made changes to the leap-year rule. February would have twenty-nine days in any year that could be evenly divided by four. The exception would be century years (those ending in 00), which would be leap years only if they could be divided by four hundred. So 1800 and 1900 were not leap years, but 2000 will be.

Pope Gregory XIII met with scholars and priests to present his ideas for fixing the calendar.

The new calendar was called the Gregorian calendar after Pope Gregory. It had eleven months of thirty or thirty-one days and one month—February— that had twenty-eight or twenty-nine days. Every four hundred years, the calendar repeats itself exactly.

The Gregorian calendar insures that the first day of spring—the vernal equinox—falls on or about March 21 each year. It is the most accurate in history except for the Maya calendar, which was far more complicated. The modern Gregorian calendar differs from the solar year by only about twenty-six seconds per year—one day every twenty-five hundred years.

George Washington

Although Catholic countries were quick to adopt the Gregorian calendar after it was created in 1582, other countries were against making the change. It was finally accepted in England and its colonies, including those in North America, in 1752. In order to make the change, however, eleven days had to be eliminated from the English calendar, so in that year, September 2 was followed by September 14. For some dates, even the year changed. This led to a great deal of confusion. According to the old calendar (Julian), George Washington was born on February 11, 1731. But on the Gregorian calendar, his birthday became February 22, 1732!

Other countries adopted the Gregorian calendar even later—Japan in 1873, China in 1912, Russian in 1918, and Greece in 1924. However, in these countries the Gregorian calendar was put into use only as a civil calendar, for governmental and business affairs. Ancient, traditional calendars continued to be used for religious purposes. China's traditional calendar matches each year with one of twelve animals—Rat, Ox, Tiger, Hare, Dragon, Serpent, Horse, Ram, Monkey, Rooster, Dog, and Boar. The year 2000 is the Year of the Dragon.

Year of the RAT	Year of the OX	Year of the TIGER	Year of the HARE	Year of the DRAGON	Year of the SERPENT
4646 / 1948	4647 / 1949	4648 / 1950	4649 / 1951	4650 / 1952	4651 / 1953
4658 / 1960	4659 / 1961	4660 / 1962	4661 / 1963	4662 / 1964	4663 / 1965
4670 / 1972	4671 / 1973	4672 / 1974	4673 / 1975	4674 / 1976	4675 / 1977
4682 / 1984	4683 / 1985	4684 / 1986	4685 / 1987	4686 / 1988	4687 / 1989
4694 / 1996	4695 / 1997	4696 / 1998	4697 / 1999	4698 / 2000	4699 / 2001
4706 / 2008	4707 / 2009	4708 / 2010	4709 / 2011	4710 / 2012	4711 / 2013

There is a traditional Chinese belief that a person's character is determined by his or her animal sign.

In the Chinese lunar calendar each year is named for an animal. Beginning with the Rat, the wheel reads counterclockwise and represents a twelve-year cycle.

RAT

BOAR

OX

DOG

TIGER

ROOSTER

鼠

猪

犬

牛

羅

虎

猴

HARE

MONKEY

段

羊

蟬

蛇

DRAGON

RAM

SERPENT

HORSE

Year of the HORSE	Year of the RAM	Year of the MONKEY	Year of the ROOSTER	Year of the DOG	Year of the BOAR
4652 / 1954	4653 / 1955	4654 / 1956	4655 / 1957	4656 / 1958	4657 / 1959
4664 / 1966	4665 / 1967	4666 / 1968	4667 / 1969	4668 / 1970	4669 / 1971
4676 / 1978	4677 / 1979	4678 / 1980	4679 / 1981	4680 / 1982	4681 / 1983
4688 / 1990	4689 / 1991	4690 / 1992	4691 / 1993	4692 / 1994	4693 / 1995
4700 / 2002	4701 / 2003	4702 / 2004	4703 / 2005	4704 / 2006	4705 / 2007
4712 / 2014	4713 / 2015	4714 / 2016	4715 / 2017	4716 / 2018	4717 / 2019

The shofar, or ram's horn, is sounded at the start of the Jewish New Year.

A muezzin calls Muslims to prayer from the minaret atop a mosque.

The Hebrew calendar is the official calendar of Israel as well as the religious calendar for Jews all over the world. Based on the Babylonian calendar, it begins in the year 3760 BC on the Gregorian calendar, which marks the time of creation in the Jewish faith, and has twelve or thirteen months of seven-day weeks. Each week ends with day seven—the Sabbath (Saturday), a day of rest.

Muslim countries also use their traditional calendar for both civil and religious purposes. The Islamic calendar dates from the Hegira, or Hijra, the journey of the prophet Muhammad from the city of Mecca to the city of Medina in the Gregorian year 622— the Muslim year AH 1 (*Anno Higerae*). This lunar calendar has twelve months, each beginning at sunset on the day the moon's crescent is sighted. Since the calendar has only 354 days, over the years the months move backward through the seasons.

On the Chinese New Year, an enormous paper dragon is paraded through the streets.

In India, a country of many religions, there have been as many as thirty calendars in use all at the same time. Despite the government's effort to change this, there are still many different calendars, including those used by Buddhists, Hindus, and Jains.

Today most of the world uses the Gregorian calendar for official business. But although it is a good calendar and everyone is used to it, some people think it is time for a new calendar—one that is not related to any religion. The Gregorian calendar is a Christian calendar, and since not even half the world's people are Christians, many feel that there is good reason for change. Some proposals would allow each religious group to use its own calendar for holy days and festivals, while using one multicultural and international calendar for the business of nations. So far, none of the proposals has been popular enough to gain acceptance. Most people don't like the idea of changing something they are so used to.

The Christian festival of Luciadagen (St. Lucia's Day) is celebrated in Sweden on December 13.

Hindus celebrate Diwali in India during the month of Kartika. It is a joyous festival of light.

33

Calendars are one way of keeping track of time—the days, weeks, months, and years. Although early humans had no need for smaller units of time, people gradually paid more attention to hours, minutes, and seconds. Clocks keep track of these smaller units of time. In today's world, most of us live our lives by the clock. It tells us when to get up, go to school or work, eat our meals, and go to bed.

The very first "clocks" kept track of time by measuring shadows. Thousands of years ago people began to notice that shadows cast by the sun changed with the time of day. They shortened around noon and lengthened toward evening. So the length of a shadow could tell people the time of day.

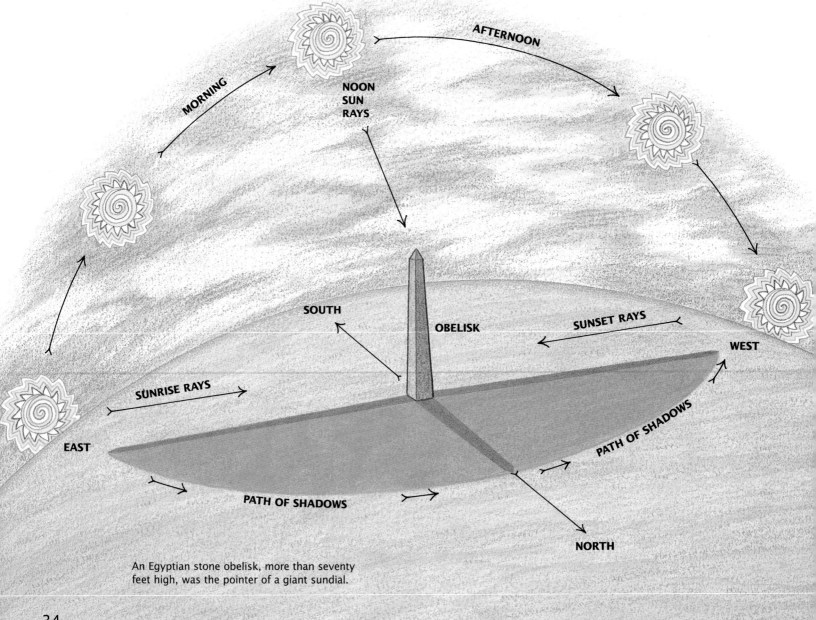

An Egyptian stone obelisk, more than seventy feet high, was the pointer of a giant sundial.

A garden sundial from eighteenth-century Europe

An hourglass

A portable sundial with compass
from fifteenth-century Europe

Sundials were first used long ago by the Sumerians, Egyptians, and Chinese. Sundials use a stick, or pointer, called a gnomon to cast a shadow on a flat surface marked with the hours. Some sundials were simple, others complicated, some very large, others small enough to fit in a pocket. However, sundials can tell the time only when the sun is shining.

Around 325 BC, water clocks began to appear in Egypt. They measured time by letting water drip slowly, at a regular rate, from one container to another. Each mark on the lower container equaled one hour. Later water clocks became very elaborate, sometimes including gongs, bells, pointers, dials, or moving figures.

Burning candles were also used to count the hours. As they burned, the markings on the candles showed how many hours had gone by. Hourglasses measured time by allowing sand to flow at a slow, even rate from one glass bulb to another.

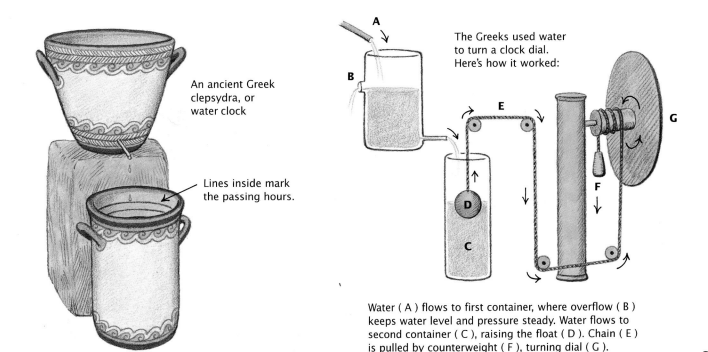

An ancient Greek clepsydra, or water clock

Lines inside mark the passing hours.

The Greeks used water to turn a clock dial. Here's how it worked:

Water (A) flows to first container, where overflow (B) keeps water level and pressure steady. Water flows to second container (C), raising the float (D). Chain (E) is pulled by counterweight (F), turning dial (G).

A European clock tower in a medieval town

Water clocks, hourglasses, and candle clocks did not depend on the sun and could be used at any time. But they weren't very accurate over days or weeks. Sometime in the 1300s, mechanical clocks began to be used in Europe, but no one knows who made the very first ones. These clocks used the pull of gravity for power. A heavy weight was attached to a cord tightly wound on a spool. As the cord unwound, it turned sets of toothed wheels called gears, which then moved the hands on the clock's face. Very large clocks of this type were set in clock towers in cities and towns.

Other clocks were powered by the action of a spring unwinding. A flat band of steel, tightly coiled, slowly unwound, moving the gears and hands. Unfortunately, none of these clocks was as accurate as people would have liked it to be. These clocks would often lose as much as fifteen minutes per day.

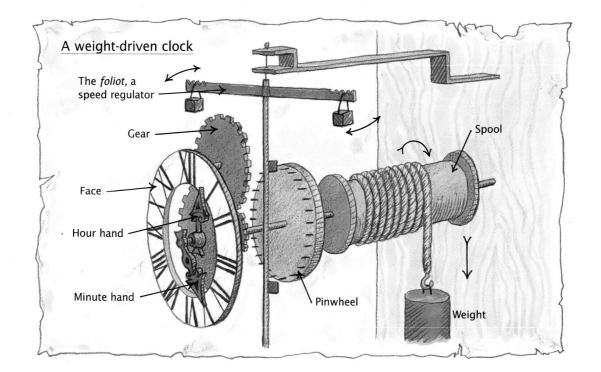

A weight-driven clock

The *foliot*, a speed regulator

Gear

Face

Hour hand

Minute hand

Pinwheel

Spool

Weight

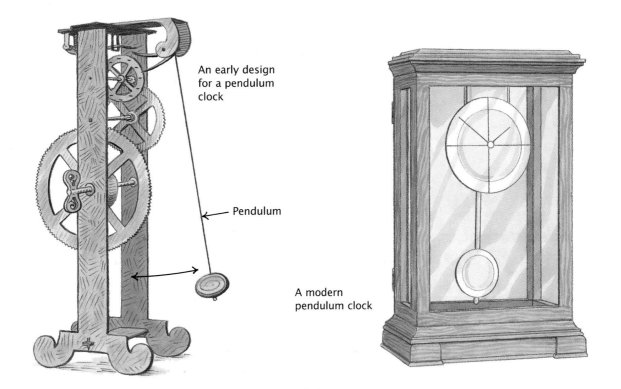

An early design
for a pendulum
clock

Pendulum

A modern
pendulum clock

Around the middle of the 1600s, more accurate pendulum clocks were invented. A swinging pendulum keeps a steady rhythm if it is kept perfectly level. The rate of the swing can be adjusted by changing the length of the pendulum. With each swing, the gears move one notch.

Although the clocks still used springs or weights, pendulums improved accuracy by providing more reliable, regular motion. Soon after they were introduced, the accuracy of pendulum clocks improved to an error of less than ten seconds per day.

Early clocks were always quite large. Over time, clock makers found ways to make timepieces smaller and smaller, until finally wearable clocks—watches— allowed people to take their clocks with them wherever they went.

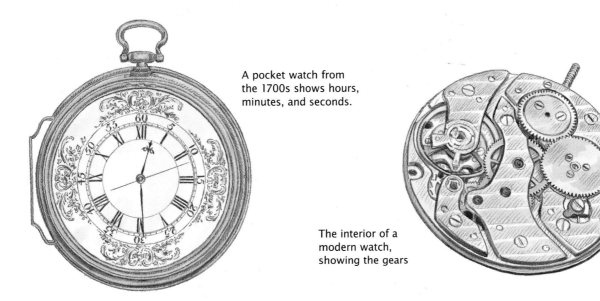

A pocket watch from
the 1700s shows hours,
minutes, and seconds.

The interior of a
modern watch,
showing the gears

But still scientists and inventors looked for ways to make clocks even more reliable and accurate. In the late 1800s, the discovery of electricity led to the invention of electrically powered clocks that were more accurate than any clocks in the past. Later, in the 1960s, convenient cordless clocks operated by battery power became popular.

Earlier in the 1900s, a search had begun to create a clock so precise that it could be used for air and sea navigation, astronomy, communications systems, and other scientific purposes. Quartz clocks that use no gears or mechanical devices seemed to be the answer. A small battery is used to send an electric current to quartz crystals inside the clock, causing them to vibrate. These vibrations deliver pulses of current—steady, precise signals controlled by a microchip—to the clock's motor. Quartz clocks are now accurate to within a tiny fraction of a second over a period of months.

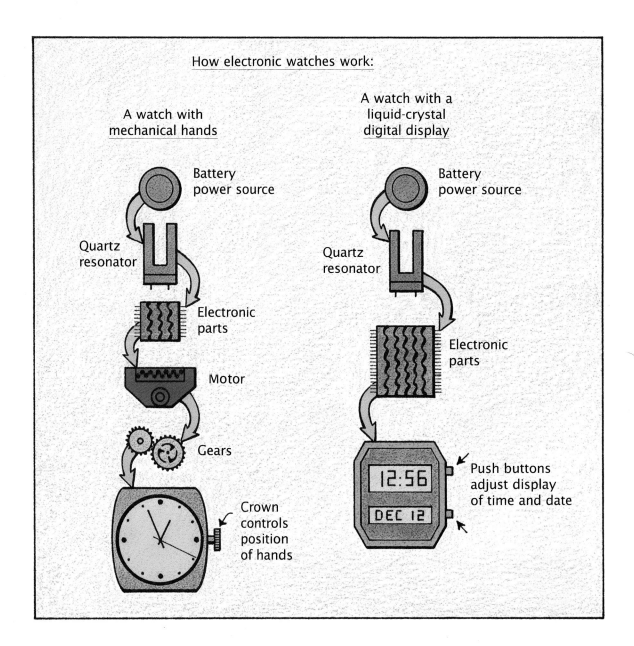

How electronic watches work:

A watch with mechanical hands

A watch with a liquid-crystal digital display

Battery power source

Quartz resonator

Electronic parts

Motor

Gears

Crown controls position of hands

Battery power source

Quartz resonator

Electronic parts

12:56

DEC 12

Push buttons adjust display of time and date

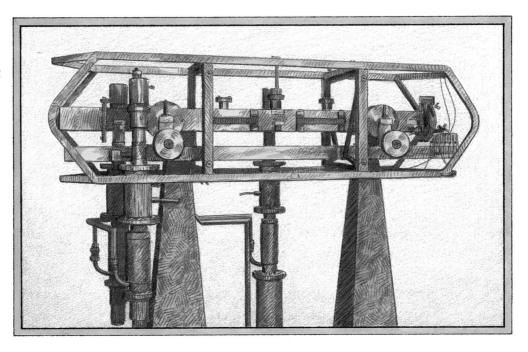

Early cesium atomic clock used before 1962

Atomic clocks are the most accurate of all. They measure time by counting the very regular vibrations—more than nine billion a second—in atoms of cesium, a natural radioactive chemical. Atomic clocks are so precise that they may have an error of only one second in millions of years! Since 1967, atomic clocks have kept the official time on earth.

A modern atomic clock

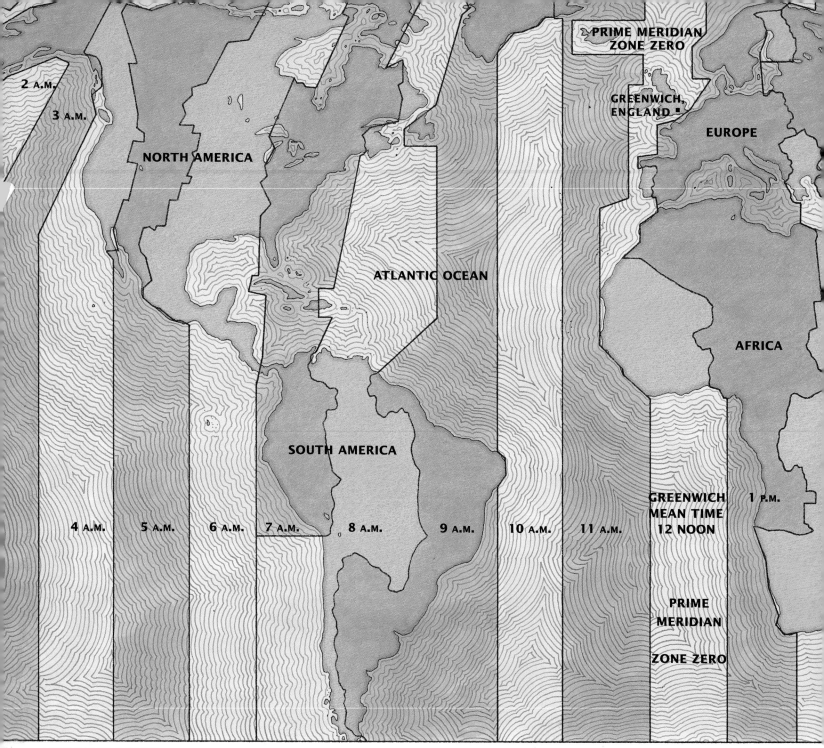

THE TIME ZONES

Because the earth rotates, different locations experience day and night at different times. About a hundred years ago, in order to regulate official timekeeping on earth, there was an international agreement to establish twenty-four time zones. Each is centered on an imaginary line called a meridian that runs north/south around the earth through the North and South Poles. Time starts at Zone Zero at the Prime Meridian in Greenwich, England. All the clocks in each time zone keep the same time, and each zone is one hour ahead of or behind the time zones on either side.

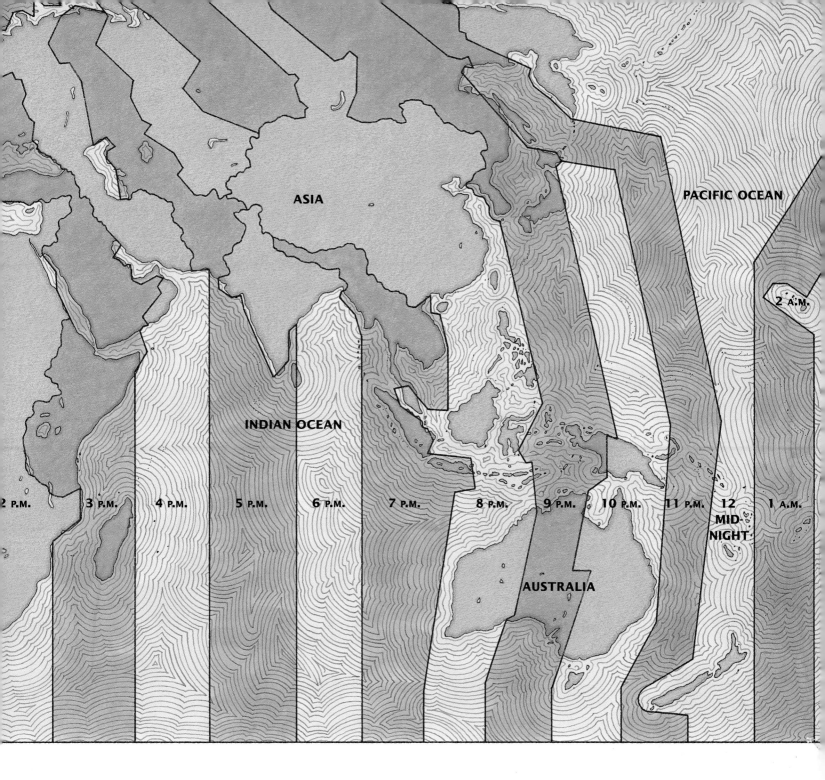

Coordinated Universal Time is the time at Zone Zero. Time zones to the east of Greenwich are later by one hour; to the west, they are earlier. Time zone boundaries have been altered a bit so that people who live in one small country, or one city, state, or region will all be on the same time. In large countries like the United States, there are a number of time zones. So when someone asks, "What time is it?" the answer depends on where you are.

The story of time has no beginning and no end that we know of. Time can't be seen or touched—in fact, no one can say exactly what time is. Yet people seem to be able to measure it. But although we may not understand just what it is, we have mastered the time of our daily lives. Calendars and clocks may not be perfect, but they are accurate enough to get most of us where we need to go on time. And clocks and calendars are still evolving—lasers and mercury atoms may provide a new generation of clocks. Who knows? Someday the world could adopt a whole new calendar system.

If we think of time in its largest sense, two thousand years may not seem very remarkable. But when we think in terms of human time, it's easy to understand why an anniversary marking two thousand years is a very special event. Although it is the year 2000 only on the Gregorian calendar, it is important to us because that is the calendar most of us use.

Although many people think that the new millennium began on January 1, 2000, the new century and the new millennium will not actually begin until January 1, 2001. Because there is no zero in Roman numerals, there never was a year 0 on the Gregorian calendar. Since the calendar began with the year AD 1, it will be two thousand years in 2001. But most people celebrated a year early—on New Year's Eve of December 31, 1999, and New Year's Day of January 1, 2000—whether or not it was correct.

Although the year 2000 is celebrated as the anniversary of the birth of Jesus Christ, religious scholars now think that Jesus was actually born four to six years earlier than was previously thought. But even if the two thousandth anniversary of His birth many have already passed, the spirit of the celebration is still very important to Christians throughout the world.

Since sunrise doesn't happen at exactly the same time everywhere on earth, lots of people are wondering where the first sunrise of the new millennium will take place. It will probably be at the Balleny Islands in Antarctica. But wherever the first sunrise is, and wherever you are, the beginning of the new millennium will be an exciting and memorable event—a once (or maybe twice, if you celebrate both dates) in a lifetime experience. The year 2000 is a very special mark in time.

THE DATE IS NOT THE SAME ON EVERY CALENDAR

Saturday, January 1, 2000	GREGORIAN	Monday, January 1, 2001
24 Ramadan 1420	ISLAMIC	5 Shawwal 1421
23 Teveth 5760	HEBREW	6 Teveth 5761
19 December 1999	JULIAN	19 December 2000
11 Dey 1378	PERSIAN	12 Dey 1379
23 Takhsas 1993	ETHIOPIAN	24 Takhsas 1994
22 Kiyahk 1716	COPTIC (Egyptian)	23 Kiyahk 1717

THE FIRST SUNRISE

There is a great deal of discussion about where on earth the first sunrise of the new millennium will be.

Some believe that the first sunrise will take place in Antarctica because that region around the South Pole has perpetual sun from September through March. During that time, the sun is below the horizon for less than one hour a day.

Another group argues that, since there are no people to see the sunrise in Antarctica, the "first sunrise" will actually be in Kiribati, a group of thirty-three Micronesian islands in the mid–Pacific Ocean north of New Zealand. The government of Kiribati is of course spreading the word in the hope of attracting tourists for the big event.

Still other interested observers insist that people along a great half-circle from eastern Russia through China, the Bay of Bengal, and Antarctica will be the ones to observe the first sunrise.

But wherever the *first* sunrise is seen, most people will watch the sun rise on the new millennium in their own backyards at the time of their own local sunrise.

ONCE IN A BLUE MOON

When people say that something happens only "once in a blue moon," they mean that it happens very rarely, only once in a great while. This expression has been used for more than one hundred years. But it appears that there really is such a thing as a blue moon: Every once in a while the moon can appear to have a bluish tint caused by ice crystals in the atmosphere, clouds, or dust storms. But a blue moon has come to mean the second full moon to occur in a single calendar month. This can happen because the moon's cycles do not always mesh with the calendar. So about seven times every nineteen years, there are two full moons in a calendar month. One year in nineteen has two blue moons because February may have no full moon at all. In 1996 there was a blue moon on July 30; in 1999 there were two of them—one on January 31 and another on March 31.

Names have been given to other moons as well. The moon was often called by a different name each month, the names differing from culture to culture. In the United States January's moon was called a wolf moon, while September's was the harvest moon. A February moon was known as the snow moon, and the strawberry moon came in June.

OTHER INTERESTING FACTS ABOUT TIME AND CALENDARS

The Pawukon calendar system is native to the island of Bali in Indonesia. It keeps the time of the rice-growing cycle, and has only six months and a year of only 210 days.

The Hebrew calendar is based on other early calendars from the Near East area that was once Mesopotamia. Hebrew month names are very similar to Mesopotamian months. The Mesopotamian Tashritu became the Hebrew Tishri; Arahsamnu, Heshvan; Kissilimu, Kislev; Tebetu, Tevet; Shabatu, Shevat; Addaru, Adar; Nisannu, Nisan; Ajaru, Iyar; Simanu, Sivan; Tamuzu, Tammuz; Abu, Av; and Ululu, Elul.

Chinese years take their character and nature from the animal associated with that year. The year 4698 is the Year of the Dragon and begins on February 5, 2000. People born in years of the dragon are said to be powerful leaders, aggressive and determined. The year 4699 is the Year of the Serpent and begins on January 24, 2001. People born in years of the serpent are said to be charming, brainy, decisive, and successful.

The Latin phrase *Carpe diem,* meaning "Seize the day," was carved on many sundials and clocks for centuries. It came to mean "Make good use of the day" and "Make every minute count"—different ways of saying that time is too precious to waste.

During the French Revolution, a reformed calendar free of religious connection was adopted and put into use in France. It began on September 22, 1792, the day the new republic was proclaimed. It had twelve months of thirty days with ten-day weeks. Month names corresponded to seasonal changes: Frimaire (frost), Florial (blossom), and Messidor (harvest) were three.

Two groups of people in the Eastern Mediterranean, the Copts and the Ethiopians, did not follow the Islamic faith and so did not adopt the Islamic calendar. The Coptic and Ethiopian churches never accepted the Gregorian calendar either. Instead, they devised their own systems. Both are 360-day calendars, the Coptic beginning in AD 284 and the Ethiopian in AD 7 on the Gregorian calendar.

By agreement of the 1884 International Meridian Conference, January 1, 2000, and January 1, 2001, will arrive everywhere around the world according to local times. But officially the new millennium will arrive at the moment of midnight in Greenwich, England, the Prime Meridian and the site of the Royal Observatory.

When the American colonies switched to the Gregorian calendar in 1752, Ben Franklin wrote, "It is pleasant for an old man to be able to go to bed on September 2 and not have to get up until September 14."

COMMON DIVISIONS OF TIME

second   one sixtieth of a minute. Since 1967 the international definition of a second is exactly 9,192,631,770 vibrations of an atom of cesium. This definition replaces the old second defined in terms of the earth's motions.

minute   sixty seconds, or one sixtieth of an hour.

hour   sixty minutes, or one twenty-fourth of a day.

day   twenty-four hours measured from midnight to midnight. Astronomers measure a day from noon to noon. Also, the period of time it takes for the earth to make one complete rotation on its axis.

week   a period of seven days.

month   a period of approximately four weeks, or about thirty days. Also, about one twelfth of a year.

year   a period of twelve months, or approximately 365 days. Also, the period of time it takes for the earth to make one complete revolution around the sun.

decade   a period of ten years.

century   a period of one hundred years.

millennium   a period of one thousand years.

DIFFERENT MEANINGS OF TIME

astronomical time   the division of time as related to astronomical events.

sidereal time   the division of time as related to the position of distant stars as observed from earth. A sidereal day is the time it takes between two passages of the same star through a particular meridian. It is 23 hours, 56 minutes, and 4.0905 seconds in length.

solar time   the division of time based on the apparent revolution of the sun around the earth. A solar day runs from noon to noon and is longer than a sidereal day by about four minutes.

ephemeris time   the division of time based on the yearly revolution of the earth around the sun. Used by astronomers to determine the exact positions of stars and planets.

Julian day   measures time as a continuous count of days beginning from a zero point of January 1, 4713 BC, at noon. The Julian date is the number of days since that starting point and is used by scientists. On January 1, 2000, the count will be 2,451,545.

apparent time   the time kept by a sundial, based on the sun's apparent position in the sky.

International Atomic Time   the time kept by a number of atomic clocks located around the world.

Coordinated Universal Time   the international time standard managed by the Bureau of International Time in France. It is based on continual comparisons of many atomic clocks in different countries. Time zones are synchronized with UTC. Sometimes used now instead of Greenwich Mean Time.

local time   the time in a particular time zone.

civil time   clock time as used for everyday purposes rather than scientific purposes.

THE NAMES OF THE DAYS OF THE WEEK

	SUN	MOON	MARS	MERCURY	JUPITER	VENUS	SATURN
English	Sunday	Monday	Tuesday	Wednesday	Thursday	Friday	Saturday
Latin	Dies Solis	Dies Lunae	Dies Martis	Dies Mercurii	Dies Jovis	Dies Veneris	Dies Saturni
Saxon	Sunnan daeg	Monan daeg	Tiwes daeg	Wodens daeg	Thors daeg	Frigg daeg	Satern daeg
French	Dimanche	Lundi	Mardi	Mercredi	Jeudi	Vendredi	Samedi
Italian	Domenica	Lunedi	Martedi	Mercoledi	Giovedi	Venerdi	Sabato
German	Sonntag	Montag	Dienstag	Mittwoch	Donnerstag	Freitag	Samstag

The original seven-day week came from the Babylonians. Their day names came from the names of their gods of the sun, the moon, and the planets. The Greeks then changed the names to those of *their* gods for the same heavenly bodies. Later the names of the Roman, Saxon, and Norse gods were substituted in each of those cultures. Most languages that stem from Latin have similar day names, just as Anglo-Saxon languages have related names.

After the founding of Christianity, some of the names for the sun's day and Saturn's day changed to reflect their religious significance. So some names for Saturday are related to Sabbath day, and many names for Sunday stem from the Latin *Domini* for "the Lord's day."

The names for sun and moon often stem from the Latin roots *sol* and *luna,* which also give us the words *solar* and *lunar.*

In German, *Mittwoch,* which means "midweek," is used for Wednesday, which does indeed fall in the middle of the week.

THE YEAR 2000 AND COMPUTERS

The coming of the year 2000 created a very big problem for the world's computer systems. As a space saver, dates have always been programmed into computers using only two digits. So 1990 is just 90, and 1999 is 99. The year 00 has always referred to 1900. Therefore, the turning of December 31, 1999, to January 1, 2000, is confusing to computers. Although the whole world knew for a very long time that this problem was approaching, programmers were slow to come up with good solutions. The problem is most serious for very large computer systems like those used by governments, banks, and large corporations and universities. A number of solutions were proposed, but by 1998 few had been implemented. No one knows exactly what will happen.

INDEX